# My Mother's Husbands

*poems by*

# Anna Gasaway

*Finishing Line Press*
Georgetown, Kentucky

# My Mother's Husbands

## ACKNOWLEDGMENTS

"Fetal Cells Found in the Mother," "Inheritance," and "Medical History"
published in the *Bipolar Body Issue of the Circus Collective*
"If There Be Any Virtue or Any Praise" in the *Los Angeles Review*
"Questions from the Angel of Death" in *Cream City Review*
"The Kenmore Refrigerator" *Mom Egg Review*
"My Mother Later Told Me That They Had Sex" in the *VOLTA Voidspace
Launch Party*
"On the Tenth Step" in *Anti-Heroin Chic*
"Trying to Describe My Mother's Relationship to Me" forthcoming in
*Frontier Poetry*

Publisher: Leah Huete de Maines
Editor: Christen Kincaid
Cover Art: Anna Gasaway & Metropolitan Museum of Art
Author Photo: Joshua R. Gasaway
Cover Design: Anna Gasaway & Elizabeth Maines McCleavy


Order online: www.finishinglinepress.com
also available on amazon.com


Author inquiries and mail orders:
Finishing Line Press
PO Box 1626
Georgetown, Kentucky 40324
USA

# Contents

## Woman Caught

Did you think they wouldn't stone me?
That the teacher would say, *Go and sin no
more*, and that would be the end of it? You have
heard it said  this was a parable about
humanity. *Whoever has not sinned—*
Did you think that they would just stop? People
like to finish what they start. First,
a smattering of pebbles from the toddlers,
then little rocks tossed as if in jest.
I looked upon the faces of the men
that I had made my husband and their wives
holding sharp stones in their hands. *It was
a righteous anger* they told themselves later.
*She had it coming.* Stabbing
pain, then nothing.

## Fetal Cells Found in Mother

*"We're walking around with a whole family tree inside of us."*
*Scientific American, 2015*

My mother in her MaryJane's and lace anklets
will forever be clattering down the church parquet
shouting that she's glad that she has a daddy
even if he's in a box; how I knew, I knew
beforehand, my baby was dead in my womb;
why I called my mother that night right before
my stroke; why her mother always preferred her over all
the others: *microchimerism*, the cells made of snippets
of all of the family tree, melding different parts
of the animal of each body.

## After the Fall

Steel mills smudge the air gray.
I follow my older sister out past
the broken ice of Lake Michigan.
Right here seems like it will hold
me. I hear a crick-crack, exhale,
*oh*. Lavender corduroyed leg
plunges through. Sister is farther
ahead, and much lighter; Father
starts speaking to me like an animal—
*Steady, girl.* He wears a frayed
plaid jacket too light for winter
weather, his wingtips ruined;
blue hand outstretched to me.

## Sonnets for My Mother's Husbands

### Tom: 1961-1964

Mom's first marriage—as an escape from
her reality, a stepfather cornering
her in the kitchen while her mother
was in an asylum where he put her;
when Mom visited her there, Grandma grabbed
onto her clothing and wouldn't let go,
chased her down the hallways of the locked ward.
Mom's husband bored her. He loved her too much,
had funny teeth; he worked hard at the steel
mill and left her with their kids and soap
operas where Erica was constantly
unfaithful—Mom wanted something more.
Her dream was to be a jazz singer on a cruise,
sparkle as she sang *The Way We Were.*

## David: 1971-1986

She met him at Moody Bible Institute
while they were being filled with the Holy
Spirit. She saw him dancing. She had never
seen anyone so free, so anointed,
(which is my mom's slang for sexy). Their first
kiss, in a dorm room where my mother was
not supposed to be, Dad describes as electric
with demonic energy. She thought he'd be rich,
weren't Jews supposed to be rich? She thought that
at least he'd be a family man, concerned
with his children, working to provide better
than he had. He listened to her. And then
he was a good talker, charismatic,
convincing people to do anything he wanted.

*

My mother later told me that they had sex
four times a day every day. Tilt-
O-Whirl rides taken to induce abortion
between me and my little brother. She
already had three babies under three and
my father hid her birth control. When
she found it and began taking it again
he denied her sex and they both started
having affairs. Where did they find the time?
She worked as a nurse at a children's home,
he sold books for Zondervan. There was us.
All I know is this: the split pea soup
that my mother's dentist's wife made for us
kids, warm and filling. The wife's pleas
for Mom to give her husband back, fading.

## Ode to Kirk
### *(April-May, 1984)*

You took my hand and we entered the skating
rink dappled with disco lights. *You just have
to go side to side, like this.* I looked down—
you held me firmly. I felt safer with you
than my own father. You were tall and lanky,
and slept on the couch after visiting
our mother.  You had a mustache and chuckled,
were the between-man, the uneducated
man, sold your furniture so we could press
quarters into Q-bert and Pacman. You
hunted wild rabbit for us—the meat sparse
and gamy. I tasted the metal, rolling
BBs around in my mouth.

*Frank: 1989-1990*

This is what I know—that Frank left her
in airport security on their honeymoon
after Mom made a joke about a bomb
that the stewardess did not find funny—
that she sang *kum-bah-yah* in jail, bringing
the love of Christ into all situations—
that my father picked her up from O'Hare
and brought her home to Regency Park,
—that he said that he would always love her—
that she said *if you would just have gotten
a job to support the children*—that he
waved her out from his tore-up VW Rabbit.

\*

Frank had a cream Chevrolet Caprice
with plush red velvet interior. He always had
a cigarette in his hands or mouth, even when
he made lasagna, even when he scrubbed the floor
and complained about my brothers' *not*. When
he went to McDonald's, he would take extra
napkins, ketchup, mustard packets, salt
and pepper shakers. He called it tax. My
mother later said that she married him
not because he made her smile, or was a good
dancer—no, she needed someone to watch
her youngest son while she worked.
He had a pile of bacon for breakfast,
and then fried his eggs in their grease. When his
doctors said, *change your diet or you don't
have long to live.* He said *if I can't eat
what I want, then I'd rather die* and did.

## Paul: 1993-1994

Paul pushed his way into my dorm room
flashing a wedding ring and baring his dentures
in a grin. He had a greasy comb-over, gray
polyester pants. *You weren't supposed to say
anything*—Mom parsed her lips. Paul said *I didn't.*
I asked, *You're married again? What do you
want? My congratulations? Are you happy?*
She nodded. *Good.* Their camper van was parked
on the red. It would have been embarrassing
had I that capacity. They were touring
witchy Salem where my mom sensed a spirit-
ual battle. She said my school was full
of demons. I said that she was full of shit.

*Where Were You in All This Drama?*

I take a scientific approach to all this—
pulling a ruby out of a velvet

bag, looking for fissures with a jeweler's
loupe, knowing what I can never have.

I prick my finger with a safety pin
and smile into a mirror. She tries to rile

me up. I react with nothing, knowing
that she cannot bear to be without

an antagonist. She wears glittery clothes,
garish jewelry—I put on varied shades

of brown. detached, alien child.

*Hush*

My mother told me that they had sex four
times a day when I was twelve before she
said *I didn't want any of you, your father*
*hid my birth control, and I give and I*
*give and I give and you take and you take*
*and you take.* I would take my younger brother
to the kidney-shaped swimming pool that
was in the center of Regency Park
by the willow tree. He would cannonball
and do flips into the water. I swam
laps and when I was done, I blew out all
of my air and sank down to the drain.
It was peaceful down there. I looked
at my tan arms and long legs. *This is what*
*it must be like to drown*, I said to myself,
*no struggle, hushed, quiet.*

## After the Divorces

When my husband and I are fighting,
my mind goes straight to divorce. It's the way
I'm wired. Then I think to myself, is that
what mom would do? And if I say yes, then
I don't do it. Walking the OB pier
with my baby boy, I had the urge to throw
myself over the side with him in my arms.
I wouldn't have to attend to his constant
colicky crying. Would my mother
do that? It's the kind of thing that she
would do, recklessly and without thinking.

\*


Alone with someone that's attractive to me,
would she come on to them? Absolutely!
She pinches her CNA's butts in the nursing
home, she aggressively goes after all men
that she meets, waiters, bus drivers, rando
guy on the street. When a surfer shakes
their curly dirty-blonde hair and grins
at me, my first response is to smile and flirt.
I ask myself, would she? And then I don't.
It's like a BASIC program that I tried
so hard to learn in seventh grade. If X,
then Y. And who am I if I am living
my life as a reverse to this woman?
It binds me to her like nothing else will.

## On the Tenth Step
*(Cento from Owl at Home)*

Tonight, I will make tear-water tea. Think
of things that were sad, never seen again.

Wind pushed Owl against the wall. Winter
made the window shades flap and shiver.

To be upstairs and downstairs at the same
time. Owl sat on the tenth step—a place

right in the middle of the edge of the sea.

## Trying to Describe My Mother's Relationship to Me

I am Batman to your Joker, Mary Ann
goody-goody to your sexy, glittery
Ginger; Bruce Banner to your Hulk smashing
everything and everyone around you;
Spock's logic to Captain Kirk's outbursts; I
am boring you say—that's what I've always
wanted. It doesn't mean that I have not
been drawn to your way of life like Jean Luc
Picard to the Borg. Your gravity terrifies
me, your attempts at assimilation are futile.

## Questions From the Angel of Death

*Exodus 12:12 when he sees the blood on the top and sides*
*of the doorframe...He will not permit his death angel to*
*enter your house and strike your first-born son.*

What about intersex people born with
both parts, should I take them too? And should I
take the babes still inside the womb? How soon?
Six weeks? And when You said to me, if
the doorposts are painted red with the blood
of a perfect lamb; what is perfect? What
if an Israelite didn't paint all the doorposts
completely? Or could not get their hands on
a lamb for slaughter? (You know how your humans
are with scarcity.) What if they couldn't
bring themselves to slit the lamb's throat? Should
I take their son? When I fly around as a thief
in the night will people think badly of me? Say
no one should lose their first-born son on a technicality?

## Inheritance

We were the chosen children, the ones she never left; who threw fits when told to nap, the ones who called her *bitch*. We thought we were alien life forms, always moving, always leaving, always saying goodbye. We were the gifted and the talented, the sons and daughters of the Most High God and the only poor Jew she ever met. We escaped into books, television and teacher's approval. When the pastor and the deacon looked a little too long at our little bodies, we were the children who had to watch our own backs. We were latchkey children, five-for-a-dollar Salisbury Steak TV Dinner eaters. We went to ballet with our grandparents and out to Chinese food and weren't supposed to tell them we couldn't afford shoes. We lined up to receive Grandpa's crisp ten-dollar bills before going back to Indiana in the rusty, wood-sided station wagon with bags of brisket and challah sandwiches. We were the children whose parents fought all the time until the blessed silence of divorce. We were the children of a mother always looking for her father.

**If there be any virtue or any praise**
*after Rick Barot*

When any word is called for, say
that I am with. When weeds grow
taller than the grass, that is persistence.
An earthquake swings the house,
that is time's pendulum. When decluttering
a room, creating a haven. When
a mosquito bites your inner ear,
this is an invitation to listen. A dog
throws up on the rug, think of curtains
snapping. When a mother poisons
herself with medications, think
relief. When a peacoat becomes frayed,
crumpled waves. When asthma closes
the throat, think Lot's wife. When seagulls
steal your last Doritos, think of sand-worn
stone. When ravens whicker, laundry.

## Medical History

*After Nicole Sealey*

I've had a stroke. I've had cancer. Three
fetuses have made their home in my womb—
one survived. I've had an abortion.
I have asthma. I'm prone to desperate
depression. I have latent TB. I'm
on blood thinners. My mother has
bipolar disorder. She almost died of COVID after
trying to kill herself at my home. At times, she
picked her hair until she was bald. At times,
I pick my skin until it bleeds. My mother's mother
died of a heart attack. My mother's father, in
World War II. My father went blind with religion
and glaucoma. My cousin died of addiction.
My son has perfect vision, although both
of us have poor eyesight. He's an experiment.
What random assortment of genes turned off
and on will he express? What will happen
to a child, when he's given all the love
and support that he wants?

## The Kenmore Refrigerator

The light's gone out but it still keeps things cold
and freezes—Sears has gone out of business,
so ten-year warranty's no good. No repair
person will come and visit this relic;
it was the cheapest version—had no frills, no
ice maker; we figured that's the first thing
that would break—but no, it was the side
shelves; they have a weak middle—we duct taped
them round and round. It's filthy with ghosts
of salad-dressings past, celery and greens
left languishing, tuna from the *Land of the Lost*,
weird smelling rot at the back. These three things
remain, our ripe avocados, my son's wax-encircled
baby bells; my husband's apples, pristine in their drawer.

**Anna Abraham Gasaway** (She/Her) is an emerging disabled writer published in *Frontier, Zone 3, Cream City Review, Poetry International, Anti-Heroin Chic, One Art* and others. She received her MFA from SDSU and serves as an editorial assistant for the Los Angeles Review. She can be found on BlueSky: @annagasaway.bsky.social; Twitter/X at @Yawp97 and IG: annagasaway.